Magnet Board Creations

LEISURE ARTS, INC. • Maumelle, Arkansas

Contents

SHOPPING LIST

Yarn (Medium Weight Yarn) MEDIUM 4

- ☐ Small amount of color of your choice.

Crochet Hook

- ☐ Size G (4 mm)

Additional Supplies

- ☐ Yarn needle
- ☐ Moveable eyes, embroidery floss, a broom, alphabet shaped pasta, a pearl, polyester stuffing, ribbon, and magnetic strips.

Refer to Basic Crochet Stitches, page 31, before beginning.

Seaside I

EASY

Octopus

OCTOPUS

Body

Rnd 1 (Right side)**:** With Lt Green, ch 2, 6 sc in second ch from hook; join with slip st to first sc.

Note: Loop a short piece of yarn around any stitch to mark Rnd 1 as **right** side.

Rnd 2: Ch 1, 2 sc in same st as joining and in each sc around; join with slip st to first sc: 12 sc.

Rnd 3: Ch 1, 2 sc in same st as joining, sc in next sc, (2 sc in next sc, sc in next sc) around; join with slip st to first sc: 18 sc.

Rnd 4: Ch 1, sc in same st as joining and in next sc, 2 sc in next sc, (sc in next 2 sc, 2 sc in next sc) around; join with slip st to first sc: 24 sc.

Arms

★ Ch 20, sc in second ch from hook and in next 11 chs, hdc in next 7 chs, slip st in next sc on Body; repeat from ★ 7 times **more;** finish off.

Weave in all yarn ends. Trim as desired, using photo as a guide.

CRAB

Body

With Rose, ch 10, sc in second ch from hook, † hdc in next 2 chs, dc in next ch, tr in next ch, dc in next ch, hdc in next 2 chs †, 3 sc in last ch; working in free loops of beginning ch ***(Fig. 3b, page 30)***, repeat from † to † once, 2 sc in same ch as first sc; join with slip st to first sc, do **not** finish off: 20 sts.

Legs & Pinchers

† Ch 8, slip st in second ch from hook and in each ch across, slip st in next st on Body †; ch 10, slip st in second ch from hook, hdc in next ch, dc in next ch, sc in next ch, skip next 2 chs, sc in next 3 chs, slip st in next hdc on Body, sc in next dc, 2 hdc in next tr, sc in next dc, slip st in next hdc; ch 7, slip st in second ch from hook, hdc in next ch, dc in next ch, 3 sc in next ch, sc in next 2 chs, slip st in next hdc on Body, repeat from † to † 3 times; ch 9, hdc in third ch from hook, dc in next ch, sc in next ch, skip next 2 chs, sc in next 2 chs, slip st in next hdc on Body, sc in next 5 sts, slip st in next hdc; ch 8, hdc in third ch from hook, dc in next ch, sc in next ch, 3 sc in next ch, sc in next 2 chs, slip st in next sc on Body, repeat from † to † once; ch 8, slip st in second ch from hook and in each ch across; join with slip st to first st, finish off.

Weave in all yarn ends. Trim as desired, using photo as a guide.

Crab

HERMIT CRAB

Hermit Crab

Shell

Rnd 1 (Right side)**:** With White, ch 2, 6 sc in second ch from hook; do **not** join, place marker to indicate the beginning of the rnd ***(see Markers, page 30).***

Note: Loop a short piece of yarn around any stitch to mark Rnd 1 as **right** side.

Rnd 2: Working in BLO ***(Fig. 2, page 30),*** 2 hdc in next sc and in each sc around: 12 hdc.

Rnd 3: Working in BLO, 2 dc in each of next 6 hdc, 2 tr in each of next 6 hdc, dc in **both** loops of next dc; finish off.

Crab

Working in both loops, join Brown with slip st in last dc on Shell, (ch 4, slip st in second ch from hook and in next 2 chs, slip st in same dc) twice; ch 8, slip st in second ch from hook and in next ch, sc in next 5 chs, slip st in end of last rnd; ch 7, slip st in second ch from hook and in next ch, sc in next 4 chs, slip st in same st as last dc worked on Rnd 3; ch 6, slip st in second ch from hook and in next ch, sc in next 3 chs, slip st in same st on Shell; ch 5, slip st in second ch from hook and in next ch, sc in next 2 chs, slip st in same st on Shell; finish off.

Weave in all yarn ends. Trim as desired, using photo as a guide.

OYSTER

Center

Row 1: With Lavender, ch 2, 3 sc in second ch from hook.

Row 2 (Right side)**:** Ch 1, turn; sc in first sc, 2 sc in next sc, sc in last sc: 4 sc.

Note: Loop a short piece of yarn around any stitch to mark Row 2 as **right** side.

Row 3: Ch 1, turn; 2 sc in first sc, sc in next 2 sc, 2 sc in last sc: 6 sc.

Row 4: Ch 1, turn; 2 sc in first sc, sc in next sc, 2 sc in each of next 2 sc, sc in next sc, 2 sc in last sc: 10 sc.

Row 5: Ch 1, turn; 2 sc in first sc, sc in next 8 sc, 2 sc in last sc: 12 sc.

Row 6: Ch 1, turn; sc in each sc across.

Row 7: Ch 1, turn; 2 sc in first sc, sc in next 4 sc, 2 sc in each of next 2 sc, sc in next 4 sc, 2 sc in last sc: 16 sc.

Row 8: Ch 1, turn; sc in first 2 sc , (sc, hdc, sc) in next sc, ★ sc in next sc, (sc, hdc, sc) in next sc; repeat from ★ 4 times more, sc in last 3 sc; finish off leaving a long end for sewing.

Shell

BOTTOM

Rows 1–7: With Variegated, work same as Center: 16 sc.

Row 8: Ch 1, turn; sc in each sc across.

Row 9: Ch 1, turn; beginning in first sc, sc2tog, sc in next 3 sc, 2 sc in next sc, (sc in next sc, 2 sc in next sc) twice, sc in next 4 sc, sc2tog, slip st in end of first row; do not finish off.

Joining: Ch 1; with **right** sides together, Bottom facing and working through both thicknesses, work 7 sc evenly spaced across end of rows; 2 sc in free loop of beginning ch ***(Fig. 3b, page 30);*** working in end of rows, work 7 sc evenly spaced across to last row on Bottom, slip st in last row; working in BLO on Bottom ***(Fig. 2, page 30),*** slip st in each st across; join with slip st to first sc, finish off.

Thread yarn needle with end, tack Center to Bottom between Rows 7 and 8 of Center; stuffing lightly before closing.

TOP

Rows 1–8: With Variegated, work same as Bottom: 16 sc.

Edging: Ch 1, turn; beginning in first sc, sc2tog, sc in next 3 sc, 2 sc in next sc, (sc in next sc, 2 sc in next sc) twice, sc in next 4 sc, sc2tog; working in end of rows, slip st in first row, ch 1, work 7 sc evenly spaced across, 2 sc in free loop of beginning ch; working in end of rows, work 7 sc evenly spaced across to last row, slip st in last row; working in BLO, slip st in each sc across; join, do **not** finish off.

Oyster

Shark

Joining: With **wrong** sides of Top and Center together, Bottom facing and working through inside loops of **each** stitch of **both** pieces; ch 1, slip st in each st across; finish off.

Weave in all yarn ends. Trim as desired, using photo as a guide.

SHARK

Body

With MC, ch 18, sc in second ch from hook and in next ch, hdc in next ch, dc in next ch, tr in next 6 chs, dc in next ch, hdc in next ch, sc in last 5 chs; do **not** finish off.

Tail Fins

With Lt Grey, ch 6, slip st in second ch from hook and in next ch, sc in next 2 chs, dc in next ch, slip st in end of Body; ch 4, slip st in second ch from hook and in next ch, hdc in next ch, slip st in first free loop of beginning ch on Body ***(Fig. 3b, page 30);*** finish off.

Belly

Working in free loops of beginning ch, join White with slip st in same st as last slip st made, sc in next 6 chs, hdc in next 2 chs, dc in next 3 chs, hdc in next 2 chs, sc in next 2 chs, slip st in last ch; finish off.

Top Fin

Join Lt Grey with slip st in eighth st on Body; ch 7, slip st in second ch from hook, sc in next ch, skip next ch, hdc in next ch, skip next ch, dc in next ch, skip next 2 sts on Body, slip st in next st; finish off.

Side Fin

With Lt Grey, ch 7, hdc in third ch from hook, dc in next ch, tr in next 3 chs; finish off leaving a long end for sewing.

Weave in all yarn ends.

Using Cover Photo as a guide for placement: Sew Side Fin to Body.

Trim as desired.

MAN-OF-WAR

Body

Rnd 1 (Right side)**:** With White, ch 2, 6 sc in second ch from hook; join with slip st to first sc.

Note: Loop a short piece of yarn around any stitch to mark Rnd 1 as **right** side.

Rnd 2: Ch 1, 2 sc in same st as joining and in each sc around; join with slip st to first sc: 12 sc.

Rnd 3: Ch 1, 2 sc in same st as joining, sc in next sc, (2 sc in next sc, sc in next sc) around; join with slip st to first sc: 18 sc.

Rnd 4: Ch 1, sc in same st as joining and in next sc, 2 sc in next sc, (sc in next 2 sc, 2 sc in next sc) around; join with slip st to first sc: 24 sc.

Rnd 5: Ch 1, 2 sc in same st as joining, sc in next 3 sc, (2 sc in next sc, sc in next 3 sc) around; join with slip st to first sc: 30 sc.

Joining: With **wrong** sides together, fold circle in half, ch 2, sc in second ch from hook, working through **both** loops of **both** pieces, sc in first 4 sc, ch 2, (2 dc in next sc, dc in next sc) twice, 2 hdc in next sc, hdc in next 2 sc, sc in next 3 sc, ch 2, sc in second ch from hook, sc in last sc; finish off.

Tentacles

Working along folded edge of Body, join Pink with slip st in last sc made; ch 11, slip st in second ch from hook and in next 3 chs, ch 2, slip st in next ch, skip next 2 chs, slip st in next ch, ch 2, slip st in next 2 chs; working in end of rnds, sc in next 2 rnds; ch 18, slip st in second ch from hook and in next 4 chs, (ch 2, slip st in next ch, skip next 2 chs, slip st in next ch) 3 times; working in end of rnds, sc in next 2 rnds; ch 20, slip st in second ch from hook and in next 4 chs, (skip next 2 chs, slip st in next ch, ch 2, slip st in next ch) 3 times, slip st in next 2 chs; working in end of rnds, sc in next 2 rnds; ch 21, slip st in second ch from hook and in next 4 chs, (ch 2, slip st in next ch, skip next 2 chs, slip st in next ch) 3 times, ch 2, slip st in next ch, ch 1, slip st in next 2 chs; working in end of rnds, sc in next rnd, slip st in next rnd; finish off.

Weave in all yarn ends. Trim as desired, using photo as a guide.

Man-O-War

Seaside II

EASY

Lobster

LOBSTER

Body

Dk Red, ch 15, sc in second ch from hook and in next ch, hdc in next 2 chs, dc in next 3 chs, sc in next 6 chs, 5 sc in last ch; working in free loops of beginning ch ***(Fig. 3b, page 30),*** sc in next 6 chs, dc in next 3 chs, hdc in next 2 chs, sc in next ch, sc in same ch as first sc.

Legs, Pinchers, & Tail

Ch 3, slip st in first 3 sts on Body; ch 9, slip st in second ch from hook, (hdc, dc) in next ch, dc in next ch, (dc, hdc) in next ch, 3 sc in next ch, sc in next 3 chs, slip st in next 2 sts on Body; **†** (ch 8, slip st in second ch from hook and in each ch across, slip st in next st on Body) 4 times **†**, slip st in next 5 sc on Body; (ch 4, hdc in third ch from hook, dc in next ch, skip next st on Body, slip st in next st on Body) twice, slip st in next 5 sts on Body, repeat from **†** to **†** once; ch 15, slip st in second ch from hook, skip next ch, hdc in next ch, (skip next ch, dc in next ch) twice, hdc in next ch, (sc in next ch, skip next ch) twice, sc in next 2 chs, slip st in next 3 sts on Body; join with slip st to first st, finish off.

Weave in all yarn ends. Trim as desired, using photo as a guide.

Three Fishes

THREE FISHES

With Pink, Aqua, or Red, ch 8, slip st in second ch from hook, ch 2, slip st in second ch from hook and in same ch as first slip st, slip st in next ch, sc in next ch, hdc in next ch, dc in next ch, hdc in next ch, slip st in last ch; finish off.

Weave in all yarn ends. Trim as desired, using photo as a guide.

STARFISH

Rnd 1 (Right side)**:** With Gold, ch 2, 5 sc in second ch from hook; join with slip st to first sc.

Note: Loop a short piece of yarn around any stitch to mark Rnd 1 as **right** side.

Rnd 2: Ch 1, 2 sc in same st as joining and in each sc around; join with slip st to first sc: 10 sc.

Rnd 3: Ch 1, 2 sc in same st as joining, sc in next sc, (2 sc in next sc, sc in next sc) around; join with slip st to first sc: 15 sc.

Rnd 4: Ch 8, hdc in third ch from hook and in next 2 chs, dc in next 3 chs, skip next 2 sc, ★ slip st in next sc; ch 8, hdc in third ch from hook and in next 2 chs, dc in next 3 chs, skip next 2 sc; repeat from ★ 3 times **more;** join with slip st to first st: 5 points.

Rnd 5: Slip st evenly around entire Starfish; join with slip st to first slip st, finish off.

Weave in all yarn ends. Trim as desired, using photo as a guide.

Starfish

MANTA RAY

Manta Ray

Rnd 1 (Right side)**:** With Dk Green, ch 9, sc in second ch from hook and in next ch, 2 dc in next ch, ch 1, sc in next ch, hdc in next 2 chs, sc in next ch, 5 sc in last ch; working in free loops of beginning ch ***(Fig. 3b, page 30),*** sc in next ch, hdc in next 2 chs, sc in next ch, ch 1, 2 dc in next ch, sc in next ch, sc in same ch as first sc, ch 3; join with slip st to BLO of first sc ***(Fig. 2, page 30):*** 26 sts.

Note: Loop a short piece of yarn around any stitch to mark Rnd 1 as **right** side.

Rnd 2: Working in BLO, sc in next 2 sts, 2 sc in next dc, hdc in next ch, dc in next 3 sts, hdc in next sc, sc in next 2 sc, 3 sc in **both** loops of next sc; working in BLO, sc in next 2 sc, hdc in next sc, dc in next 3 sts, hdc in next ch, 2 sc in next dc, sc in next 2 sts, slip st in next sc and in next ch, ch 1, hdc in next ch, slip st in next ch; join with slip st in **both** loops of first sc: 30 sts.

Rnd 3: Working in both loops, sc in same st as joining and in next 4 sts, (hdc, dc) in next dc, 2 tr in next dc, (dc, hdc) in next dc, sc in next hdc, ch 2, slip st in second ch from hook, sc in next 2 sc, slip st in next sc; ch 10, slip st in second ch from hook and in next 3 chs, sc in next 5 chs, skip next sc, slip st in next sc, sc in next 2 sc, ch 2, slip st in second ch from hook, sc in next hdc, (hdc, dc) in next dc, 2 tr in next dc, (dc, hdc) in next dc, sc in next 5 sts, slip st in next st; finish off.

Weave in all yarn ends.

Using Cover Photo as a guide for placement: Add accent lines to front by whipstitching in free loops of Rnd 2 ***(Fig. 3a, page 30)*** with Pink.

Trim as desired.

SEA ANEMONE

Body

Row 1 (Right side)**:** Ch 7, sc in second ch from hook and in next 2 chs, hdc in next 2 chs, dc in last ch: 6 sts.

Note: Loop a short piece of yarn around any stitch to mark Row 1 as **right** side.

Row 2: Ch 2, turn; working in BLO ***(Fig. 2, page 30),*** dc in first dc, hdc in next 2 hdc, sc in last 3 sc.

Row 3: Ch 1, turn; working in FLO ***(Fig. 2, page 30),*** sc in first 3 sc, hdc in next 2 hdc, dc in last dc.

Row 4: Ch 2, turn; working in BLO, dc in first dc, hdc in next 2 hdc, sc in last 3 sc.

Edging: Ch 1, turn; working in both loops, sc in first 5 sts, 3 sc in last st; work 7 sc evenly spaced across end of rows; working in free loops of beginning ch ***(Fig. 3b, page 30),*** 3 sc in first ch, sc in next 4 chs, 3 sc in next ch; work 3 sc evenly spaced across end of rows, 2 sc in same st as first sc; join with slip st to first sc, do not finish off.

Tentacles

Turn; ch 6, slip st in second ch from hook, sc in next 4 chs, (slip st in FLO of next sc on Edging; ch 6, slip st in second ch from hook, sc in next 4 chs) 6 times, turn; working in free loops of Edging behind Tentacles just made ***(Fig. 3a, page 30),*** slip st in next st; (ch 6, slip st in second ch from hook, sc in next 4 chs, slip st in next st) 5 times; finish off.

Weave in all yarn ends. Trim as desired, using photo as a guide.

Sea Anemone

Island Escape

EASY

SEAHORSE

Body

With Dk Green, ch 42, sc in second ch from hook and in next 2 chs, hdc in next ch, dc in next 2 chs, (skip **next** ch, YO, insert hook in **next** ch, YO and pull up a loop, YO and draw through 2 loops on hook) 4 times, YO and draw through all 5 loops on hook, skip next ch, dc in next ch, tr in next 3 chs, 2 dtr in next ch, 2 tr in next ch, dc in next 2 chs, (skip next ch, YO, insert hook in next ch, YO and pull up a loop, YO and draw through 2 loops on hook) twice, YO and draw through all 3 loops on hook (hdc in next ch, skip next ch) twice, (sc in next ch, skip next ch) 4 times, slip st in last 2 chs: 26 sts.

Edging: Ch 1; working in free loops of beginning ch ***(Fig. 3b, page 30)***, slip st in first 3 chs, (ch 1, slip st in next 2 chs) 7 times, ch 1, slip st in next ch, (slip st, ch 3, dc, ch 3, slip st) in next ch, (slip st in next 2 chs, ch 1) 8 times, slip st in next 6 chs; working across Body, slip st in first 6 sts, skip next st, slip st in next 2 sts, (sc in next st, ch 1, slip st in sc just made) 3 times, slip st in last 14 sts; join with slip st to first slip st, finish off.

Weave in all yarn ends. Trim as desired, using photo as a guide.

ISLAND IN THE SUN

Island

Row 1 (Right side)**:** With Gold, ch 15, sc in second ch from hook and in each ch across: 14 sc.

Note: Loop a short piece of yarn around any stitch to mark Row 1 as **right** side.

Row 2: Ch 1, turn; sc in each sc across to last 2 sc, sc2tog: 13 sc.

Row 3: Ch 1, turn; beginning in first sc, sc2tog, sc in next 5 sc; working in FLO ***(Fig. 2, page 30),*** sc in next 2 sc, sc in **both** loops of last 4 sc: 12 sc.

Row 4: Ch 1, turn; slip st in first sc , (ch 1, slip st in next 2 sc) 5 times, ch 1, slip st in last sc; finish off.

Water

Row 1: With **right** side facing and working in free loops of beginning ch ***(Fig. 3b, page 30),*** join Aqua with slip st in first ch; ch 1, 2 sc in same ch as joining, sc in each ch across to last ch at base of last sc, 2 sc in ch: 16 sc.

Row 2: Ch 1, turn; working in BLO ***(Fig. 2, page 30),*** sc in first sc, ★ skip next sc, (slip st, 2 sc, slip st) in next sc; repeat from ★ across to last sc, sc in last sc; finish off leaving a long end for sewing.

Fold Row 2 (waves) to front of Island and tack in place.

Tree Trunk

With **wrong** side facing, join Brown with slip st in second free loop on Row 3 of Island; ch 14, sc in second ch from hook and in next 5 chs, hdc in next 7 chs, slip st in next free loop on Row 3; finish off leaving a long end for sewing.

Tack bottom of Tree Trunk to Island.

Leaves

With **right** side facing, join Green with slip st in top of Tree Trunk.

First Leaf: Ch 7, slip st in second ch from hook, sc in next 2 chs, slip st in next 3 chs, slip st in same st on Tree Trunk.

Second Leaf: Ch 8, slip st in second ch from hook, sc in next 3 chs, slip st in next 3 chs, slip st in same st on Tree Trunk.

Third Leaf: Ch 9, slip st in second ch from hook, sc in next 4 chs, slip st in next 3 chs, slip st in same st on Tree Trunk.

Fourth Leaf: Work same as Third Leaf.

Fifth Leaf: Work same as Second Leaf.

Sixth Leaf: Work same as First Leaf; finish off.

Using Cover Photo as a guide for placement: Work French knots ***(Fig. 10, page 31)*** at base of leaves for coconuts with two strands of Tan.

Weave in all yarn ends. Trim as desired, using photo as a guide.

SPONGE AND FISH

Sponge and Fish

Sponge Base

Rnd 1 (Right side)**:** With Gold, ch 5, 3 sc in second ch from hook, sc in next 2 chs, 3 sc in last ch; working in free loops of beginning ch ***(Fig. 3b, page 30),*** sc in next 2 chs; do **not** join, place marker to indicate the beginning of the rnd ***(see Markers, page 30):*** 10 sc.

Note: Loop a short piece of yarn around any stitch on Rnd 1 to mark **right** side.

Rnd 2: Working in BLO ***(Fig. 2, page 30),*** (sc, hdc) in next sc, (hdc, sc) in next sc, (sc, hdc) in next sc, sc in next sc, hdc in next sc, (hdc, sc) in next sc, 2 sc in next sc, 2 hdc in next sc, sc in last 2 sc: 16 sts.

Rnd 3: Working in BLO, 2 sc in next sc, 2 hdc in each of next 2 hdc, 2 sc in each of next 2 sc, 2 hdc in next hdc, sc in next sc, hdc in next hdc, 2 hdc in next hdc, 2 sc in each of next 2 sc, (sc, hdc) in next sc, 2 hdc in next hdc, (hdc, sc) in next hdc, sc in next sc, hdc in next sc, slip st in next sc.

Note: Begin working in rows.

Row 1: Ch 1, turn; working in FLO ***(Fig. 2, page 30),*** sc in first 3 sts.

Row 2: Ch 1, turn; working in both loops, 2 sc in first sc, sc in next sc, 2 sc in last sc; finish off.

Trim: Working in free loops of Rnds 1 and 2 ***(Fig. 3a, page 30),*** join Gold with slip st in free loop of first st on Rnd 1; (ch 3, slip st in next st) around to beginning of Rnd 3; working in FLO, (ch 2, slip st in next st) 3 times, (ch 3, slip st in next st) 3 times, (ch 2, slip st in next st) 9 times, (ch 3, slip st in next st) 5 times, (ch 2, slip st in next st) 4 times; finish off.

Weave in all yarn ends.

Make one Fish and sew to Sponge if desired, using photo as a guide

Fish

With Aqua, ch 8, slip st in second ch from hook, ch 2, slip st in second ch from hook and in same ch as first slip st, slip st in next ch, sc in next ch, hdc in next ch, dc in next ch, hdc in next ch, slip st in last ch; finish off.

Weave in all yarn ends. Trim as desired, using photo as a guide.

SAND DOLLAR, LARGE AND SMALL

Sand Dollars

Large Top

Rnd 1 (Right side)**:** With White, ch 2, 6 sc in second ch from hook; join with slip st to first sc.

Note: Loop a short piece of yarn around any stitch to mark Rnd 1 as **right** side.

Rnd 2: Ch 1, 2 sc in same st as joining and in each sc around; join with slip st to first sc: 12 sc.

Rnd 3: Ch 1, 2 sc in same st as joining, sc in next sc, (2 sc in next sc, sc in next sc) around; join with slip st to first sc: 18 sc.

Rnd 4: Ch 1, sc in same st as joining and in next sc, 2 sc in next sc, (sc in next 2 sc, 2 sc in next sc) around; join with slip st to first sc: 24 sc.

Rnd 5: Ch 1, 2 sc in same st as joining, sc in next 3 sc, (2 sc in next sc, sc in next 3 sc) around; join with slip st to first sc: 30 sc.

Rnd 6: Hdc in next sc, sc in next sc, 2 sc in next sc, sc in next sc, hdc in next sc, (slip st in next sc, hdc in next sc, sc in next sc, 2 sc in next sc, sc in next sc, hdc in next sc) around; join with slip st to first hdc, finish off.

Using Cover Photo as a guide for placement and using Tan, add accent lines to Top using Lazy Daisy Stitch ***(Fig. 9, page 31).***

Large Bottom

Rnds 1–6: Work same as Top; do **not** finish off.

Joining: With **wrong** sides together and Top facing, working through **both** thicknesses, slip st in st one rnd **below** same st, slip st through inside loops of next 6 sts, (slip st in st one rnd **below** next st, slip st through inside loops of next 6 sts) around, stuffing lightly before closing; join with slip st to first st, finish off.

Weave in all yarn ends. Trim as desired, using photo as a guide.

Small Top

Rnd 1 (Right side)**:** With White, ch 2, 7 sc in second ch from hook; join with slip st to first sc.

Rnd 2: Ch 1, 2 sc in same st as joining and in each of next 5 sc, sc in last sc; join with slip st to first sc: 13 sc.

Rnd 3: Ch 1, 2 sc in same st as joining, (sc in next sc, 2 sc in next sc) around; join with slip st to first sc: 20 sc.

Rnd 4: Hdc in next sc, 2 sc in next sc, hdc in next sc, (slip st in next sc, hdc in next sc, 2 sc in next sc, hdc in next sc) around; join with slip st to first hdc, finish off.

Using Cover Photo as a guide for placement and using Tan, add accent lines to Top using Lazy Daisy Stitch ***(Fig. 9, page 31).***

Small Bottom

Rnds 1–4: Work same as Top; do **not** finish off .

Joining: With **wrong** sides together and Top facing, working through **both** thicknesses, slip st in st one rnd **below** same st, slip st through inside loops of next 4 sts, (slip st in st one rnd **below** next st, slip st through inside loops of next 4 sts) around, stuffing lightly before closing; join with slip st to first st, finish off.

Weave in all yarn ends. Trim as desired, using photo as a guide.

SHELL

Top

Row 1: With Grey, ch 2, 3 sc in second ch from hook.

Row 2 (Right side)**:** Ch 1, turn; sc in first sc, 2 sc in next sc, sc in last sc: 4 sc.

Row 3: Ch 1, turn; 2 sc in first sc, sc in next 2 sc, 2 sc in last sc: 6 sc.

Row 4: Ch 1, turn; 2 sc in first sc, sc in next sc, 2 sc in each of next 2 sc, sc in next sc, 2 sc in last sc: 10 sc.

Row 5: Ch 1, turn; 2 sc in first sc, sc in next 8 sc, 2 sc in last sc: 12 sc.

Edging: Ch 1, turn; 3 sc in first sc, sc in each sc across to last sc, 3 sc in last sc; work 5 sc evenly spaced across end of rows, 2 sc in free loop of beginning ch ***(Fig. 3b, page 30);*** work 5 sc evenly spaced across end of rows; join with slip st to BLO of first sc ***(Fig. 2, page 30),*** finish off.

Bottom

Work same as Top; do **not** finish off.

Joining: With **wrong** sides together and Bottom facing, working through inside loops of **each** stitch of **both** pieces, slip st in each sc around, stuffing lightly before closing; join with slip st to first slip st, finish off.

Weave in all yarn ends. Trim as desired, using photo as a guide.

MAGNET BOARD CREATIONS

Desert Delights

EASY

LONE COYOTE

Background

Row 1 (Right side)**:** With Blue, ch 15, sc in second ch from hook and in each ch across: 14 sc.

Note: Loop a short piece of yarn around any stitch to mark Row 1 as **right** side.

Rows 2–13: Ch 1, turn; sc in each sc across.

Finish off.

Coyote

Body and Muzzle: With Rust, ch 11, sc in second ch from hook and in each ch across; ch 3, working in back ridge of chs ***(Fig. 1, page 30),*** slip st in second ch from hook, sc in last ch; working in free loops of beginning ch ***(Fig. 3b, page 30),*** slip st in first ch, (sc, hdc) in next ch, (hdc, sc) in next ch, slip st in next ch, (sc, hdc) in next ch, dc in next 2 chs, 2 tr in next ch, dc in next ch, hdc in last ch; do not finish off.

Tail and Foot: Ch 10, sc in second ch from hook and in next 3 chs, hdc in next 3 chs, 2 sc in each of last 2 chs; sc in side of last hdc on Body, sc in same ch as last hdc on Body, sc in first sc on Body; ch 3, working in back ridge of chs, slip st in second ch from hook, sc in last ch, slip st in **both** loops of next sc on Body; finish off leaving a long end for sewing.

Ear: With Rust and leaving a long end for sewing, ch 2, slip st in second ch from hook, ch 1; finish off leaving a long end for sewing and attach to Body.

Add Black French knot nose and eye ***(Fig. 10, page 31).***

Moon

Rnd 1 (Right side)**:** With Yellow, ch 2, 6 sc in second ch from hook; join with slip st to first sc.

Note: Mark Rnd 1 as **right** side.

Rnd 2: Ch 1, 2 sc in same st as joining and in each sc around; join with slip st to first sc: 12 sc.

Rnd 3: Ch 1, 2 sc in same st as joining, sc in next sc, (2 sc in next sc, sc in next sc) around; join with slip st to first sc, finish off leaving a long end for sewing.

Cactus

Large: With Green, ch 4, sc in second ch from hook, hdc in next ch, 5 hdc in last ch; working in free loops of beginning ch, hdc in next ch, (sc, slip st) in last ch; finish off leaving a long end for sewing.

Small: With Green, ch 4, slip st in second ch from hook, sc in next ch, 4 sc in last ch; working in free loops of beginning ch, sc in next ch, slip st in last ch; finish off leaving a long end for sewing.

Flower *(Make 2)*

With Red, ch 2, slip st in second ch from hook, (ch 1, slip st in same ch as first slip st) 4 times; finish off.

Add Yellow French Knot center to each Flower.

Attach all pieces to Background.

Weave in all yarn ends. Trim as desired, using photo as a guide.

BLUEBIRD

Bluebird

Body

Row 1: With Blue, ch 2, 4 sc in second ch from hook.

Row 2 (Right side)**:** Ch 1, turn; 2 sc in first sc and in each sc across: 8 sc.

Note: Loop a short piece of yarn around any stitch to mark Row 2 as **right** side.

Row 3: Ch 1, turn; 2 sc in first sc, sc in next sc, (2 sc in next sc, sc in next sc) across: 12 sc.

Note: Begin working in rounds.

Rnd 1: Ch 1, turn; 2 sc in first sc, sc in next 2 sc, place marker in sc just made for Branch placement, 2 sc in next sc, sc in next 2 sc, 2 sc in next sc, sc in next 3 sc, (hdc, dc) in next sc, place marker around dc just made for Beak placement, hdc in same st, (hdc, sc) in last sc; slip st evenly across end of rows; join with slip st to first sc, finish off.

Beak: Join Yellow with slip st in marked dc; ch 1, slip st in same st; finish off.

Wing

Row 1: With Blue, ch 2, (sc, 4 hdc, 2 dc) in second ch from hook: 7 sts.

Row 2 (Right side): Ch 1, turn; slip st in first dc, (ch 1, slip st in next st) across; finish off leaving a long end for sewing and attach to Body.

Note: Mark Row 2 as **right** side.

Tree

Branch: With Brown, ch 5, slip st in BLO of marked sc on Body ***(Fig. 2, page 30)*** and in BLO of next 6 sc.

Twigs: Ch 3, turn; slip st in second ch from hook and in next ch, slip st in BLO of next st; ch 3, slip st in second ch from hook and in next ch; working in BLO, slip st in st at base of ch-3 and in next 6 sts on Branch, slip st in last 5 chs; finish off.

With Yellow, add feet between Body and Branch.

Leaf: Join Green with slip st in st at end of Twig; ★ ch 4, slip st in second ch from hook, sc in next ch, slip st in next ch, slip st in same st as joining on Twig; repeat from ★ 2 times **more;** finish off.

Repeat for second Leaf.

Add 4 Red French knots to each Leaf ***(Fig. 10, page 31)***.

Weave in all yarn ends. Trim as desired, using photo as a guide.

CACTUS

Rnd 1 (Right side)**:** With Green, ch 15, sc in second ch from hook and in next 12 chs, 4 sc in last ch; working in free loops of beginning ch ***(Fig. 3b, page 30),*** sc in next 12 chs, 3 sc in same ch as first sc; join with slip st to first sc: 32 sc.

Rnd 2: Ch 1, sc in same st as joining and in next 4 sc; ch 10, hdc in third ch from hook and in next 3 chs, skip next ch, hdc2tog, skip last ch, sc in side of sc made before ch-10, skip next sc, slip st in next sc, sc in next 6 sc, 2 sc in each of next 4 sc, sc in next 5 sc; ch 10, hdc in third ch from hook and in next 5 chs, 3 hdc in next ch, 2 hdc in last ch, hdc in side of sc made before ch-10, skip next sc, slip st in next sc, sc in next 5 sc, 2 sc in each of last 3 sc, sc in same st as first sc; join with slip st to first sc.

Rnd 3: Slip st in next 4 sc; working in free loops of first ch-10, sc in first ch, 2 sc in each of next 2 chs, sc in next 5 chs, slip st in next 2 chs, slip st in each st around to next ch-10; working in free loops of ch-10, slip st in next 9 chs, 2 sc in next ch, sc in next 9 hdc, 2 sc in next hdc, sc in next 2 hdc, slip st in each st around; join with slip st to first sc, finish off.

Sand

Row 1 (Right side)**:** With Tan, ch 10, hdc in third ch from hook and in each ch across: 9 sts.

Note: Mark Row 1 as **right** side.

Row 2: Ch 1, turn; slip st in first hdc, (ch 1, slip st in next st) 8 times; finish off leaving a long end for sewing.

Sew to bottom of Cactus.

Weave in all yarn ends. Trim as desired, using photo as a guide.

Cactus

ROBIN

Body

Row 1: With Brown, ch 2, 4 sc in second ch from hook.

Row 2 (Right side)**:** Ch 1, turn; 2 sc in first sc and in each sc across: 8 sc.

Note: Loop a short piece of yarn around any stitch to mark Row 2 as **right** side.

Row 3: Ch 1, turn; 2 sc in first sc, sc in next sc, (2 sc in next sc, sc in next sc) across: 12 sc.

Note: Begin working in rounds.

Rnd 1: Ch 1, turn; 2 sc in first sc, sc in next 2 sc, place marker in sc just made for Branch placement, sc in next sc; drop Brown, with Orange, sc in same st and in next 2 sc, 2 sc in next sc, sc in next sc; cut Orange, with Brown, sc in next 2 sc, (hdc, dc) in next sc, place marked in dc just made for Beak placement, hdc in same st, (hdc, sc) in last sc, slip st evenly across end of rows; join with slip st to first sc, finish off.

Beak: Join Yellow with slip st in marked dc; ch 1, slip st in same st; finish off.

Wing

Row 1: With Brown, ch 2, (sc, 4 hdc, 2 dc) in second ch from hook: 7 sts.

Row 2 (Right side)**:** Ch 1, turn; slip st in first dc, (ch 1, slip st in next st) across; finish off leaving a long end for sewing and attach to Body.

Note: Mark Row 2 as **right** side.

Tree

Branch: With Green, ch 5, slip st in BLO of marked sc on Body ***(Fig. 2, page 30)*** and in BLO of next 6 dc.

Robin

Twigs: Ch 4, turn; slip st in second ch from hook and in next 2 chs, slip st in BLO of next st; ch 5, slip st in second ch from hook and in next 3 chs; working in BLO, slip st in st at base of ch-5 and in next 6 sts on Branch, slip st in last 5 chs; finish off.

With Dk Yellow, add feet between Body and Branch.

Leaf: Join Green with slip st in st at end of Twig; ★ ch 4, slip st in second ch from hook, sc in next ch, slip st in next ch, slip st in same st as joining on Twig; repeat from ★ 2 times **more;** finish off.

Repeat for second Leaf.

Flower *(Make 2)*

Rnd 1: With Blue, ch 2, 6 sc in second ch from hook; join with slip st to first sc.

Rnd 2: Ch 3, (slip st in next st, ch 3) around; join with slip st at base of beginning ch-3, finish off leaving a long end for sewing.

Add Yellow French knot center to each Flower ***(Fig. 10, page 31).***

Attach one Flower to each Twig.

Weave in all yarn ends. Trim as desired, using photo as a guide.

Spooky Autumn

EASY

SCAREDY CAT

Background

Row 1 (Right side)**:** With Grey, ch 15, sc in second ch from hook and in each ch across: 14 sc.

Note: Loop a short piece of yarn around any stitch to mark Row 1 as **right** side.

Rows 2–13: Ch 1, turn; sc in each sc across.

Finish off.

Grass

Row 1: With **right** side facing and working in free loops of beginning ch ***(Fig. 3b, page 30),*** join Green with slip st in first ch; ch 1, sc in same ch and in next 13 chs: 14 sc.

Row 2: Ch 1, turn; work 2 Loop Sts in first sc ***(Figs. 5a-c, page 30),*** work Loop St in each sc across to last sc, work 2 Loop Sts in last sc; finish off.

Cat

Body: With Black, ch 13, sc in second ch from hook and in next 3 chs, 2 sc in each of next 4 chs, sc in last 4 chs: 16 sc.

Tail: Turn; slip st in first 5 sc, ch 11, slip st in second ch from hook, skip next ch, slip st in next ch, skip next ch, slip st in next 4 chs, skip next ch, slip st in last ch and in next sc on Body; sc in next sc, 2 sc in each of next 2 sc, sc in next sc, leave remaining sc unworked.

Head: Ch 1, turn; (sc, hdc, 3 dc, hdc, sc, slip st) in first sc, leave remaining sts unworked.

Ears: Ch 1, turn; skip first slip st, slip st in next 2 sts; ch 2, slip st in second ch from hook 2 sts; ch 2, slip st in second ch from hook and in last 3 sts, slip st in same st as first sc, slip st in next 6 sts and in end of Body; working in free loops of beginning ch, slip st in each ch across and in end of Body; join with slip st to first slip st, finish off leaving a long end for sewing.

Trim as desired, using photo as a guide.

Pumpkin

Rnd 1 (Right side)**:** With Orange, ch 2, 6 sc in second ch from hook; join with slip st to first sc.

Note: Mark Rnd 1 as **right** side.

Rnd 2: Ch 1, 2 sc in same st as joining, 2 hdc in next sc, 2 sc in each of next 2 sc, 2 hdc in next sc, (2 sc, slip st) in last sc; do **not** join, finish off leaving a long end for sewing.

Stem: With Green, insert hook in sp **between** first and last sc on Rnd 1, YO and pull up a loop; ch 4, slip st in second ch from hook and in next 2 chs, slip st in same st as joining; finish off.

Moon

Rnd 1 (Right side)**:** With Yellow, ch 2, 6 sc in second ch from hook; join with slip st to first sc.

Note: Mark Rnd 1 as **right** side.

Rnd 2: Ch 1, 2 sc in same st as joining and in each sc around; join with slip st to first sc: 12 sc.

Rnd 3: Ch 1, 2 sc in same st as joining, sc in next sc, (2 sc in next sc, sc in next sc) around; join with slip st to first sc, finish off leaving a long end for sewing.

Bat

With Black, ch 9, slip st in second ch from hook, 2 sc in next ch, slip st in next ch, sc2tog, slip st in next ch, 2 sc in next ch, slip st in last ch; finish off leaving a long end for sewing.

Attach all pieces to Background.

Weave in all yarn ends. Trim as desired, using photo as a guide.

RIP

SPOOKY NIGHT

Background

Row 1 (Right side)**:** With Black, ch 15, sc in second ch from hook and in each ch across: 14 sc.

Note: Loop a short piece of yarn around any stitch to mark Row 1 as **right** side.

Rows 2–13: Ch 1, turn; sc in each sc across.

Finish off.

Grass

Row 1: With **right** side facing and working in free loops of beginning ch ***(Fig. 3b, page 30),*** join Green with slip st in first ch; ch 1, sc in same ch and in next 13 chs: 14 sc.

Row 2: Ch 1, turn; work 2 Loop Sts in first sc ***(Figs. 5a-c, page 30),*** work Loop St in each sc across to last sc, work 2 Loop Sts in last sc; finish off.

Tombstone

Row 1 (Right side)**:** With Grey, ch 6, sc in second ch from hook and in next 3 chs, 3 sc in last ch; working in free loops of beginning ch, sc in next 4 chs: 11 sc.

Row 2: Ch 1, turn; sc in first 4 sc, 2 sc in each of next 3 sc, sc in last 4 sc: 14 sc.

Spooky Night

Row 3: Ch 1, turn; slip st in first sc and in each sc across; finish off leaving a long end for sewing.

Moon

Rnd 1 (Right side)**:** With Yellow, ch 2, 6 sc in second ch from hook; join with slip st to first sc.

Note: Mark Rnd 1 as ***right*** side.

Rnd 2: Ch 1, 2 sc in same st as joining and in each sc around; join with slip st to first sc: 12 sc.

Rnd 3: Ch 1, 2 sc in same st as joining, sc in next sc, (2 sc in next sc, sc in next sc) around; join with slip st to first sc, finish off leaving a long end for sewing.

Ghost

With White, ch 7, slip st in second ch from hook, 2 sc in next ch, sc in next 2 chs, ch 2, slip st in top of sc just made, sc in next ch, (slip st, sc, 3 hdc, sc, slip st) in last ch; working in free loops of beginning ch, sc in next ch, ch 2, slip st in top of sc just made, sc in next ch, slip st in last 3 chs; finish off leaving a long end for sewing.

Bat

With Black, ch 9, slip st in second ch from hook, 2 sc in next ch, slip st in next ch, sc2tog, slip st in next ch, 2 sc in next ch, slip st in last ch; finish off leaving a long end for sewing.

Attach all pieces to Background.

Weave in all yarn ends. Trim as desired, using photo as a guide.

Note: Uncooked alphabet shaped pasta, highlighted with a black marker, was used for "R I P."

Pumpkins

PUMPKINS

Large

FIRST HALF

Row 1 (Right side)**:** With Orange, ch 8, sc in second ch from hook and in next ch, hdc in next ch, dc in next ch, hdc in next ch, sc in last 2 sc: 7 sts.

Note: Loop a short piece of yarn around any stitch to mark Row 1 as **right** side.

Row 2: Ch 1, turn; sc in first 2 sc, 2 hdc in next hdc, dc in next dc, 2 hdc in next hdc, sc in last 2 sc; finish off: 9 sts.

SECOND HALF

Row 1: Working in free loops of beginning ch ***(Fig. 3b, page 30),*** join Orange with slip st in first ch; ch 1, sc in same ch and in next ch, hdc in next ch, dc in next ch, hdc in next ch, sc in last 2 chs: 7 sts.

Row 2: Ch 1, turn; sc in first 2 sc, 2 hdc in next hdc, dc in next dc, 2 hdc in next hdc, sc in last 2 sc; do not finish off: 9 sts.

Edging: Ch 1, turn; sc evenly around; join with slip st to first sc, finish off.

STEM

Row 1 (Right side)**:** With Green, ch 5, slip st in second ch from hook and in next 3 chs; ch 1, 4 sc in same ch as last slip st: 8 sts.

Row 2: Ch 1, turn; 2 sc in each of first 4 sc: 8 sc.

Row 3: Ch 2, turn; skip first sc, slip st in next sc, (ch 2, skip next sc, slip st in next sc) across; finish off leaving a long end for sewing and attach to top of Pumpkin.

Small

Rnd 1 (Right side)**:** With Orange, ch 2, 6 sc in second ch from hook; join with slip st to first sc.

Note: Mark Rnd 1 as **right** side.

Rnd 2: Ch 1, 2 sc in same st as joining, 2 hdc in next sc, 2 sc in each of next 2 sc, 2 hdc in next sc, 2 sc in last sc; join with slip st to first sc: 12 sts.

Rnd 3: Ch 1, sc in same st as joining, 2 sc in next sc, 2 hdc in each of next 2 hdc, 2 sc in next sc, sc in next 2 sc, 2 sc in next sc, 2 hdc in each of next 2 hdc, 2 sc in next sc, sc in last sc; join with slip st to first sc, finish off.

STEM

Row 1 (Right side)**:** With Green, ch 4, slip st in second ch from hook and in next 2 chs, ch 1, 4 sc in same ch as last slip st.

Row 2: Ch 1, turn; slip st in first sc, (ch 1, slip st in next sc) 3 times; finish off leaving a long end for sewing and attach to top of Pumpkin.

With **right** sides facing and bottoms even, tack Pumpkins together.

Weave in all yarn ends. Trim as desired, using photo as a guide.

MAGNET BOARD CREATIONS

Falling Leaves

EASY

AUTUMN LEAVES

Leaf One

One

Rnd 1 (Right side)**:** Ch 11, sc in second ch from hook, hdc in next ch, dc in next 2 chs, tr in next ch, dc in next 2 chs, hdc in next ch , sc in next ch, 3 sc in last ch; working in free loops of beginning ch ***(Fig. 3b, page 30),*** sc in next ch, hdc in next ch, dc in next 2 chs, tr in next ch, dc in next 2 chs, hdc in next ch, sc in same ch as first sc; join with slip st to first sc: 21 sts.

Note: Loop a short piece of yarn around any stitch to mark Rnd 1 as **right** side.

Rnd 2: Ch 1, 2 sc in same st as joining, 2 hdc in next hdc, 2 dc in each of next 2 dc, 2 hdc in each of next 2 sts, sc in next 4 sts, 2 sc in next sc, sc in next 4 sts, 2 hdc in each of next 2 sts, 2 dc in each of next 2 dc, 2 hdc in next hdc, 2 sc in last sc; join with slip st to first sc: 34 sts.

Rnd 3: Slip st in next 3 sc, ch 1, (slip st in next 2 sts, ch 1) 7 times, slip st in same sc as last st and in next 2 sts, ch 1, (slip st in next 2 sts, ch 1) 6 times, slip st in next 3 sts; ch 6, slip st in second ch from hook and in each ch across; slip st in same st as ch-6, finish off.

Two

Rnd 1 (Right side)**:** Ch 6, sc in second ch from hook and in next 3 chs, 3 sc in last ch; working in free loops of beginning ch, sc in next 3 chs, 2 sc in same ch as first sc; join with slip st to first sc: 12 sc.

Note: Mark Rnd 1 as **right** side.

Rnd 2: Ch 3, 2 dc in same st as joining and in next sc, hdc in next 2 sc, sc in next sc, 3 sc in next sc, sc in next sc, hdc in next 2 sc, 2 dc in next sc, (2 dc, ch 3, slip st) in next sc, sc in last sc; join with slip st to first ch of beginning ch-3: 25 sts.

Leaf Two

Rnd 3: Ch 1, sc in same st as joining and in next 2 chs, 2 hdc in next dc, 2 dc in each of next 2 dc, dc in next dc, hdc in next 3 sts, sc in next sc, 3 sc in next sc, sc in next sc, hdc in next 3 sts, dc in next dc, 2 dc in each of next 2 dc, 2 hdc in next dc, sc in next 3 chs, sc in last sc; join with slip st to first sc: 32 sts.

Rnd 4: Slip st in next 2 sc, (ch 1, slip st in next 2 sts) 6 times, (slip st, ch 2, slip st) in next sc, slip st in next 3 sts, ch 1, (slip st in next 2 sts, ch 1) 5 times, slip st in last 3 sc; ch 6, slip st in second ch from hook and in next 4 chs, slip st in same st as ch-6; finish off.

Leaf Three

Three

Rnd 1 (Right side)**:** Ch 6, sc in second ch from hook and in next 3 chs, 3 sc in last ch; working in free loops of beginning ch, sc in next 3 chs, 2 sc in same ch as first sc; join with slip st to first sc: 12 sc.

Note: Mark Rnd 1 as **right** side.

Rnd 2: Ch 1, (sc, hdc) in same st as joining, 2 dc in next sc, (2 tr, ch 3, slip st) in next sc, sc in next 2 sc, (sc, 2 hdc, sc) in next sc, sc in next 2 sc, (slip st, ch 3, 2 tr) in next sc, 2 dc in next sc, (hdc, sc) in next sc, sc in last sc; join with slip st to first sc: 29 sts.

Rnd 3: Ch 1, sc in same st as joining and in next hdc, (hdc in next st, 2 hdc in next st) twice, (2 hdc, sc) in first ch, slip st in next 2 chs and in next sc, sc in next 2 sc, (sc, hdc, dc) in next hdc, (hdc, 2 sc) in next hdc, sc in next 2 sc, slip st in next sc and in next 2 chs, (sc, 2 hdc) in next ch, (2 hdc in next st, hdc in next st) twice, sc in last 3 sts; join with slip st to first sc: 43 sts.

Rnd 4: (Slip st in next 2 sts, ch 1) 3 times, slip st in next 3 sts, ch 2, slip st in second ch from hook, slip st in same hdc as last st and in next 3 sts, skip next st, (slip st in next 2 sts, ch 1) twice, slip st in next dc, ch 2, slip st in second ch from hook, slip st in next 2 sts, (ch 1, slip st in next 2 sts) twice, skip next st, slip st in next 3 sts, ch 2, slip st in second ch from hook, slip st in same hdc as last st, (slip st in next 2 sts, ch 1) 3 times, slip st in next 4 sts; ch 6, slip st in second ch from hook and in next 4 chs, slip st in same st as ch-6; finish off.

Weave in all yarn ends.

ACORN

Nut

Row 1 (Right side)**:** With Brown, ch 5, sc in second ch from hook and in next 2 chs, 3 sc in last ch; working in free loops of beginning ch ***(Fig. 3b, page 30),*** sc in next 3 chs: 9 sts.

Note: Loop a short piece of yarn around any stitch to mark Row 1 as **right** side.

Row 2: Ch 1, turn; sc in first 3 sc, 2 sc in each of next 3 sc, sc in last 3 sc: 12 sc.

Note: Begin working in rounds.

Rnd 1: Ch 1, turn; sc in first 3 sc, 2 sc in next sc, (sc in next sc, 2 sc in next sc) twice, sc in next 3 sc, 3 sc in next sc; work 3 sc evenly spaced across end of rows, 2 sc in same sc as first sc; join with slip st to first sc: 22 sc.

Rnd 2: Slip st in next 6 sc, (slip st, ch 1, slip st) in next sc, slip st in last 14 sc; join with slip st to first st, finish off.

Cap

Row 1: With Tan, ch 2, 3 sc in second ch from hook.

Row 2 (Right side)**:** Ch 1, turn; 2 sc in first sc, sc in next sc, 2 sc in last sc: 5 sc.

Note: Mark Row 2 as **right** side.

Row 3: Ch 1, turn; 2 sc in first sc, sc in next 3 sc, 2 sc in last sc: 7 sc.

Edging: Ch 1, turn; sc in first 6 sc, 3 sc in next sc; sc in end of next 2 rows, (sc, ch 4, slip st in second ch from hook and in next 2 chs, sc) in free loop of beginning ch, sc in end of next 2 rows, 2 sc in same st as first sc; join with slip st to first sc, finish off leaving a long end for sewing and attach to Nut.

Leaf

Rnd 1 (Right side)**:** With Variegated, ch 6, 2 sc in second ch from hook, sc in next 3 chs, 3 sc in last ch; working in free loops of beginning ch, sc in next 3 chs, sc in same st as first sc; join with slip st to first sc: 12 sc.

Note: Mark Rnd 1 as **right** side.

To work Picot, (Sc, ch 1, slip st in top of sc just made, sc) in st indicated.

Rnd 2: Ch 1, sc in same st as joining, (work Picot in next sc, slip st in next sc) twice, work Picot in each of next 3 sc, (slip st in next sc, work Picot in next sc) twice, sc in same st as first sc; ch 4, slip st in second ch from hook and in next 2 chs; join with slip st to first sc, finish off and attach to Cap.

Weave in all yarn ends.

Unforgettable Summer

EASY

REDBIRD

Redbird

Body

Row 1: With Red, ch 2, 4 sc in second ch from hook.

Row 2 (Right side)**:** Ch 1, turn; 2 sc in first sc and in each sc across: 8 sc.

Note: Loop a short piece of yarn around any stitch to mark Row 2 as **right** side.

Row 3: Ch 1, turn; 2 sc in first sc, sc in next sc, (2 sc in next sc, sc in next sc) across: 12 sc.

Note: Begin working in rounds.

Rnd 1: Ch 1, turn; 2 sc in first sc, sc in next 2 sc, place marker around sc just made for Branch placement, 2 sc in next sc, sc in next 2 sc, 2 sc in next sc, sc in next 3 sc, hdc in next sc, drop Red; with Black, dc in same st, place marker around dc just made for Beak placement; cut Black, with Red, hdc in same st and in last sc, ch 1, slip st in top of hdc just made, sc in same st; slip st evenly across end of rows; join with slip st to first sc, finish off.

Beak: Join Dk Yellow with slip st in marked dc; ch 1, slip st in same st; finish off.

Wing

Row 1: With Red, ch 2, (sc, 4 hdc, 2 dc) in second ch from hook: 7 sts.

Row 2 (Right side)**:** Ch 1, turn; slip st in first dc, (ch 1, slip st in next st) across; finish off leaving a long end for sewing and attach to Body.

Note: Mark Row 2 as **right** side.

Tree

Branch: With Brown, ch 5, slip st in BLO of marked sc on Body and in BLO of next 6 dc.

Twigs: Ch 4, turn; slip st in second ch from hook and in next 2 chs, slip st in BLO of next st; ch 5, slip st in second ch from hook and in next 3 chs; working in BLO, slip st in st at base of ch-5 and in next 6 sts on Branch, slip st in last 5 chs; finish off.

With Dk Yellow, add feet between Body and Branch.

Leaf: Join Green with slip st in st at end of Twig; ★ ch 4, slip st in second ch from hook, sc in next ch, slip st in next ch, slip st in same st as joining on Twig; repeat from ★ 2 times **more;** finish off.

Repeat for second Leaf.

Flower *(Make 2)*

Rnd 1: With White, ch 2, 6 sc in second ch from hook; join with slip st to first sc.

Rnd 2: Ch 3, (slip st in next st, ch 3) around; join with slip st at base of beginning ch-3, finish off leaving a long end for sewing.

Add Yellow French knot center to each Flower ***(Fig. 10, page 31)***.

Attach one Flower to each Twig.

Weave in all yarn ends. Trim as desired, using photo as a guide.

U.S.A.

U.S.A.

"U"

Row 1: With Red, ch 20, sc in second ch from hook and in next 7 chs, 2 sc in each of next 3 chs, sc in last 8 chs: 22 sc.

Note: Begin working in rounds.

Rnd 1 (Right side)**:** Ch 1, turn; sc in first 8 sc, 2 sc in next sc, (sc in next sc, 2 sc in next sc) twice, sc in next 8 sc, (sc, slip st) in last sc, slip st in end of Row 1; working in free loops of beginning ch ***(Fig. 3b, page 30)***, slip st in each ch across, slip st in end of Row 1 and in end of Rnd 1; join with slip st to first sc, finish off.

Note: Loop a short piece of yarn around any stitch to mark Rnd 1 as **right** side.

"S"

Rnd 1 (Right side)**:** With White, ch 19, sc in second ch from hook and in next 2 chs, 2 sc in each of next 3 chs, sc in next ch, skip next ch, sc2tog ***(see Decreases, page 31),*** skip next ch, sc in next ch, skip next ch, sc2tog, sc in last 3 chs, slip st in side of sc just made; working in free loops of beginning ch, (slip st, ch 1, sc) in first ch, sc in next 2 chs, 2 sc in next ch, sc in next ch, 2 sc in next ch, sc in next 5 chs, slip st in last 7 chs; join with slip st to first sc.

Note: Mark Rnd 1 as **right** side.

Note: Begin working in rows.

Row 1: Ch 1, sc in same st as joining and in next 2 sc, (2 sc in next sc, sc in next sc) 3 times, slip st in next 2 sc, sc2tog, slip st in next 3 sc; finish off.

"A"

Row 1: With Blue, ch 20, sc in second ch from hook and in next 8 chs, 3 sc in next ch, sc in last 9 chs: 21 sts.

Note: Begin working in rounds.

Rnd 1 (Right side)**:** Ch 1, turn; sc in first 10 sc, 3 sc in next sc, sc in last 10 sc, slip st in end of Row 1; working in free loops of beginning ch, slip st in first 5 chs, ch 3, skip next 9 chs, slip st in last 5 chs and in end of Row 1; join with slip st to first sc, finish off.

Weave in all yarn ends.

ELEPHANT

Row 1 (Right side)**:** Ch 10, slip st in second ch from hook, sc in next ch and in each ch across: 9 sts.

Note: Loop a short piece of yarn around any stitch to mark Row 1 as **right** side.

Row 2: Ch 1, turn; sc in first 8 sc, slip st in last st.

Row 3: Ch 1, turn; sc in first 7 sts, leave remaining 2 sc unworked: 7 sc.

Rows 4–6: Ch 1, turn; sc in each sc across.

Rows 7: Ch 1, turn; sc in each sc across; add on 2 sc ***(Fig. 6, page 31):*** 9 sc.

Row 8: Ch 1, turn; sc in each sc across.

Row 9: Ch 1, turn; sc in first 5 sc, leave remaining 4 sc unworked: 5 sc.

Row 10: Ch 1, turn; sc in first 4 sc, slip st in last sc.

Row 11: Ch 1, turn; slip st in first st, sc in next 4 sc; ch 5, sc in second ch from hook and in next 3 chs, slip st in side of sc made before ch-5 (trunk); slip st evenly around Body to beginning of last row; finish off.

Tail: Cut a length of yarn approximately 15" (38 cm) long and fold in half. With **right** side facing, insert hook in st at upper right corner, draw folded end through st, using both ends, ch 5, finish off. Knot end and trim to ½" (12 mm), then fray.

Ear: Ch 4, (sc, hdc) in second ch from hook, 2 dc in next ch, (hdc, sc, slip st) in last ch; finish off leaving a long end for sewing.

Sew in place on Row 9 of Body.

Weave in all yarn ends. Trim as desired, using photo as a guide.

Elephant

GENERAL INSTRUCTIONS

Abbreviations

BLO	Back Loop(s) Only
ch(s)	chain(s)
cm	centimeters
dc	double crochet(s)
dtr	double treble crochet(s)
FLO	Front Loop(s) Only
hdc	half double crochet(s)
hdc2tog	half double crochet 2 together
mm	millimeters
Rnd(s)	Round(s)
sc	single crochet(s)
sc2tog	single crochet 2 together
st(s)	stitch(es)
tr	treble crochet(s)
YO	yarn over

Symbols & Terms

★ — work instructions following ★ as many **more** times as indicated in addition to the first time.

† to † — work all instructions from first † to second † **as many** times as specified.

( ) — work enclosed instructions **as many** times as specified by the number immediately following **or** work all enclosed instructions in the stitch or space indicated **or** contains explanatory remarks.

colon (:) — the number(s) given after a colon at the end of a row or round denote(s) the number of stitches or spaces you should have on that row or round.

Gauge

The instructions for our Mood Minis are written for Medium Weight Yarn and that is what we used for our "Minis" but, if that is not handy, used Light Weight Yarn - doubled. Gauge doesn't matter that much; your Minis can certainly be a little bigger, or smaller, without changing the overall effect.

CROCHET TERMINOLOGY

United States		International
slip stitch (slip st)	=	single crochet (sc)
single crochet (sc)	=	double crochet (dc)
half double crochet (hdc)	=	half treble crochet (htr)
double crochet (dc)	=	treble crochet (tr)
treble crochet (tr)	=	double treble crochet (dtr)
double treble crochet (dtr)	=	triple treble crochet (ttr)
triple treble crochet (tr tr)	=	quadruple treble crochet (qtr)
skip	=	miss

CROCHET HOOKS

United States	Metric (mm)
B-1	2.25
C-2	2.75
D-3	3.25
E-4	3.5
F-5	3.75
G-6	4

United States	Metric (mm)
7	4.5
H-8	5
I-9	5.5
J-10	6
K-10½	6.5
L-11	8

United States	Metric (mm)
M/N-13	9
N/P-15	10
P/Q	15
Q	16
S	19

BASIC	Projects using basic stitches. May include basic increases and decreases.
EASY	Projects may include simple stitch patterns, color work, and/or shaping.
INTERMEDIATE	Projects may include involved stitch patterns, color work, and/or shaping.
COMPLEX	Projects may include complex stitch patterns, color work, and/or shaping using a variety of techniques and stitches simultaneously.

Yarn Weight Symbol & Names	LACE 0	SUPER FINE 1	FINE 2	LIGHT 3	MEDIUM 4	BULKY 5	SUPER BULKY 6	JUMBO 7
Type of Yarns in Category	Fingering, size 10 crochet thread	Sock, Fingering, Baby	Sport, Baby	DK, Light Worsted	Worsted, Afghan, Aran	Chunky, Craft, Rug	Super Bulky, Roving	Jumbo, Roving
Crochet Gauge* Ranges in Single Crochet to 4" (10 cm)	32-42 sts**	21-32 sts	16-20 sts	12-17 sts	11-14 sts	8-11 sts	6-9 sts	5 sts and fewer
Advised Hook Size Range	Steel*** 6 to 8, Regular hook B-1	B-1 to E-4	E-4 to 7	7 to I-9	I-9 to K-10½	K-10½ to M/N-13	M/N-13 to Q	Q and larger

*GUIDELINES ONLY: The chart above reflects the most commonly used gauges and hook sizes for specific yarn categories.

** Lace weight yarns are usually crocheted with larger hooks to create lacy openwork patterns. Accordingly, a gauge range is difficult to determine. Always follow the gauge stated in your pattern.

*** Steel crochet hooks are sized differently from regular hooks–the higher the number, the smaller the hook, which is the reverse of regular hook sizing.

Markers

Markers are used to help distinguish the beginning of each round being worked. Place a 2" (5 cm) scrap piece of yarn before the first stitch of each round, moving the marker after each round is complete.

Back Ridge

Work only in loops indicated by arrows ***(Fig. 1)***.

Fig. 1

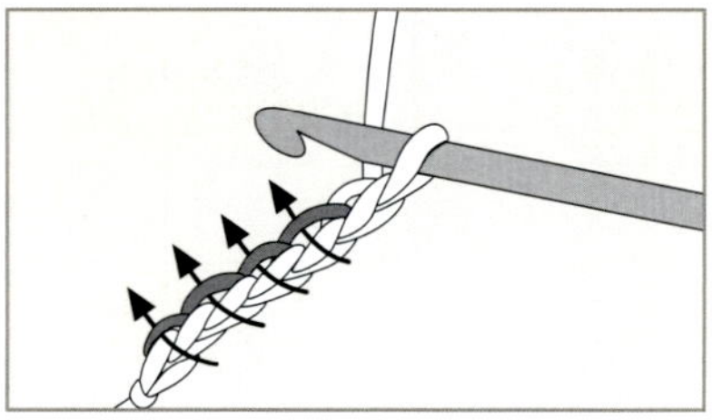

Back or Front Loop Only

Work only in loop(s) indicated by arrow ***(Fig. 2)***.

Fig. 2

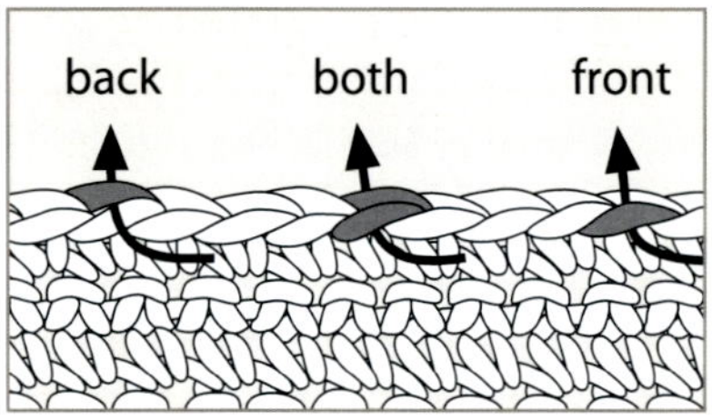

Free Loops

After working in Back of Front Loops Only on a row or round, there will be a ridge of unused loops. These are called the free loops. Later, when instructed to work in the free loops of the same row or round, work in these loops ***(Fig. 3a)***.

When instructed to work in free loops of a chain, work in loop indicated by arrow ***(Fig. 3b)***.

Fig. 3a

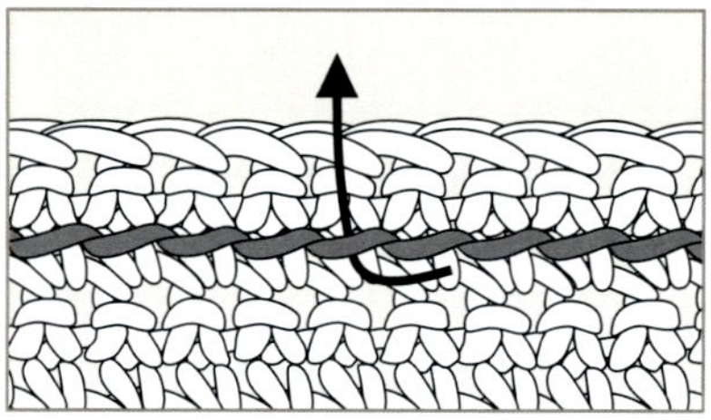

Fig. 3b

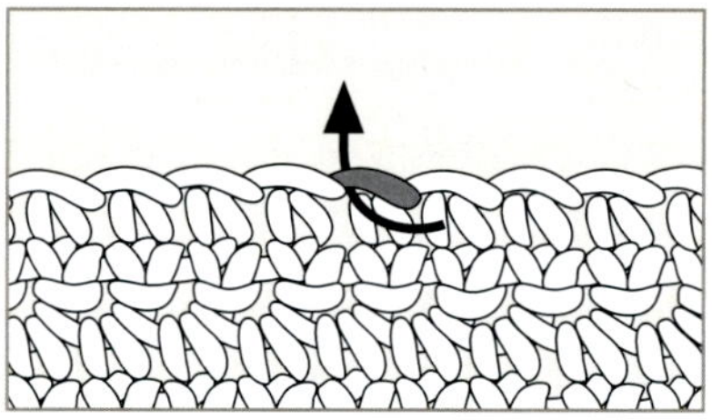

Changing Colors

Work the last stitch to within one step of completion, hook new yarn and draw through all loops on hook ***(Fig. 4)***. Do **not** cut yarn unless otherwise instructed.

Fig. 4

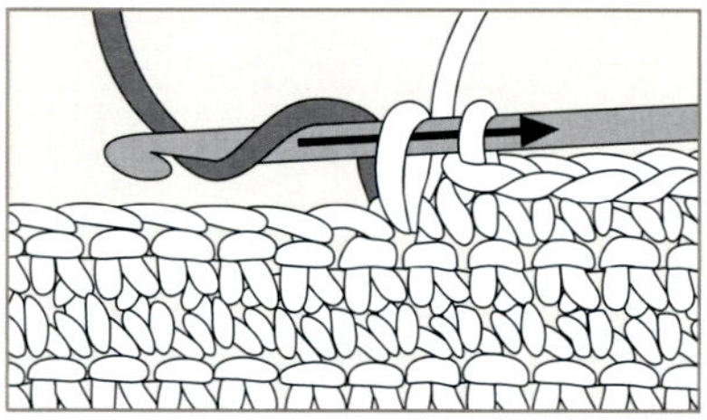

Loop Stitch

Insert the hook in the next stitch, wrap the yarn around the index finger of your left hand once **more**, insert the hook through both loops on your finger following the direction indicated by the arrow ***(Fig. 5a)***, being careful to hook all threads ***(Fig. 5b)***, draw loops through stitch, remove your finger from the loops, YO and draw through all 3 loops on the hook **(Loop St made, *Fig. 5c*)**.

Fig. 5a

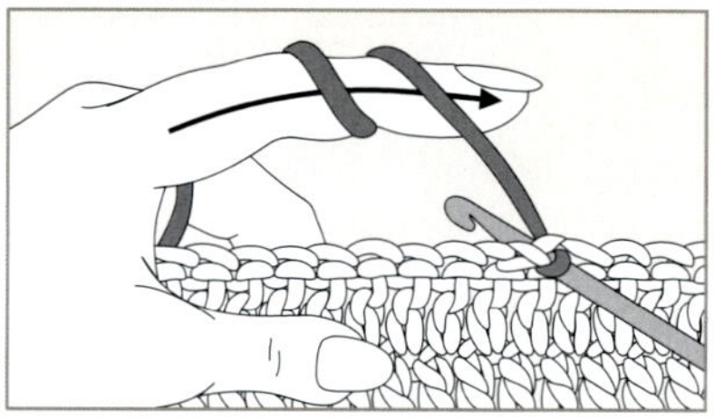

Fig. 5b

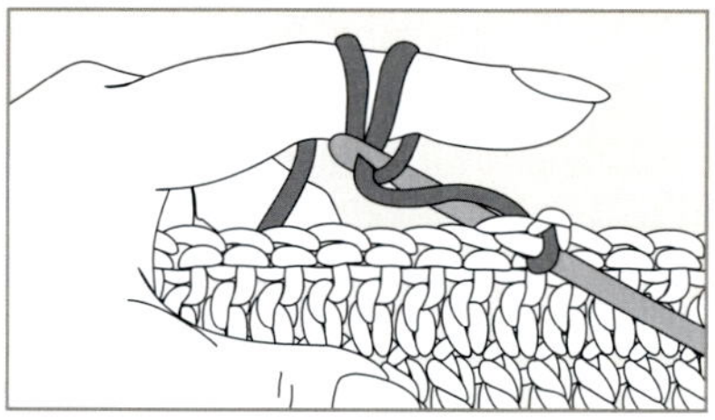

Fig. 5c

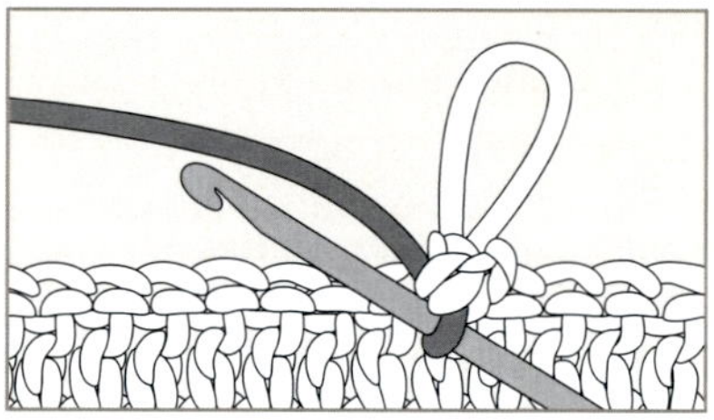

Adding Single Crochets

When instructed to add on sc, insert the hook in the base of the sc just made ***(Fig. 6)***, YO and pull up a loop, YO and draw through one loop on the hook, YO and draw through both loops on the hook. Repeat as many times as instructed.

Fig. 6

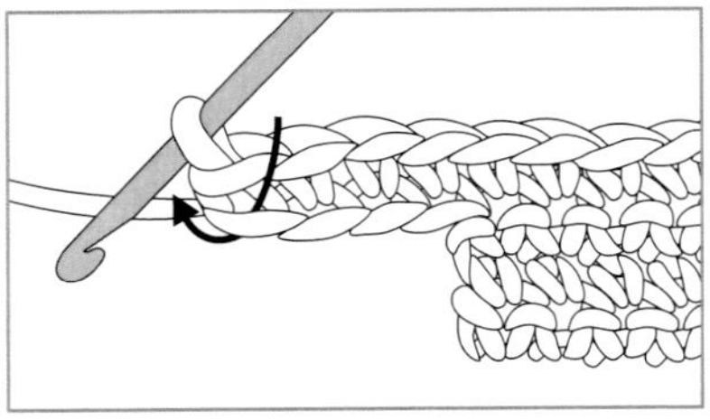

Decreases

Single Crochet 2 Together
(abbreviated sc2tog)

Pull up a loop in each of next 2 sts, YO and draw through all 3 loops on hook **(counts as one sc)** ***(Figs. 7a & b)***.

Fig. 7a

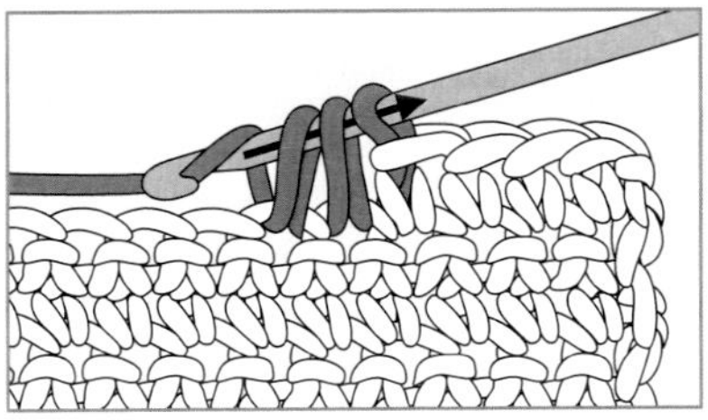

Fig. 7b

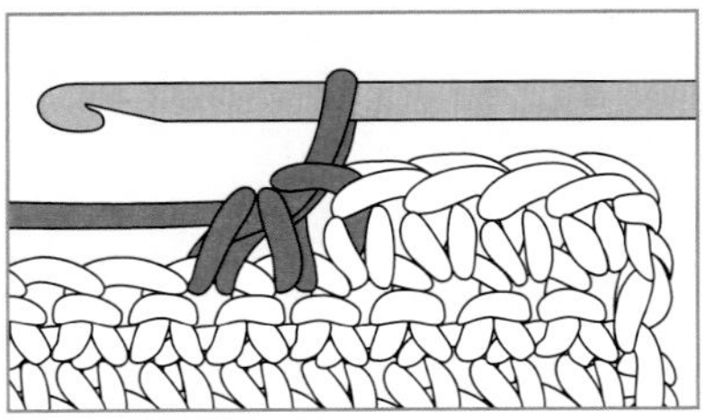

Half Double Crochet 2 Together
(abbreviated hdc2tog)

★ YO, insert hook in **next** st, YO and pull up a loop; repeat from ★ once **more**, YO and draw through all 5 loops on hook **(counts as one hdc)** ***(Figs. 8a & b)***.

Fig. 8a

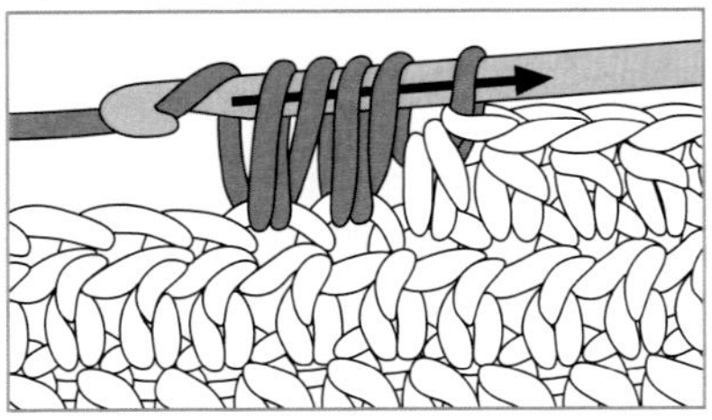

Fig. 8b

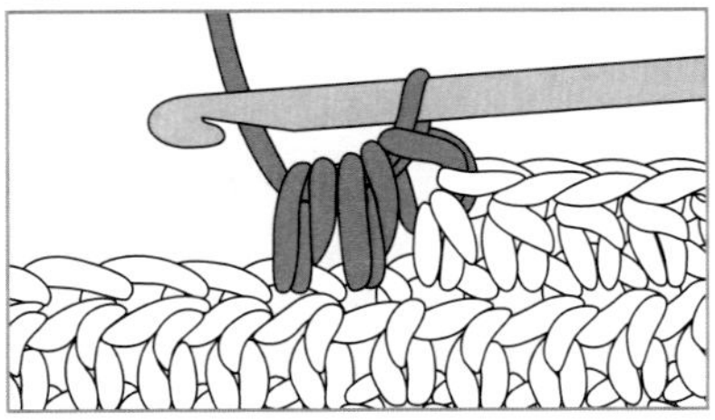

Embroidery Stitches

Lazy Daisy Stitch

Make all loops equal in length. Come up at 1 and make a counterclockwise loop with the yarn. Go down at 1 and come up at 2, keeping the yarn below the point of the needle ***(Fig. 9)***. Secure the loops by bringing the yarn over the loop and down at 3. Repeat for remaining accent lines.

Fig. 9

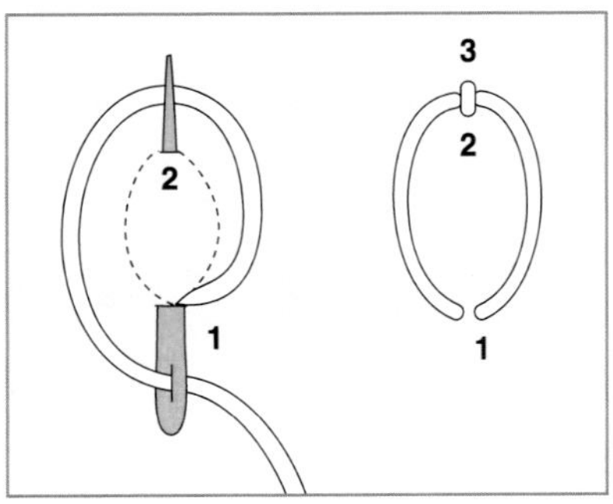

French Knot

Bring the needle up at 1. Wrap the yarn around the needle once and insert the needle at 2, holding the end of the yarn with your non-stitching fingers ***(Fig. 10)***. Tighten the knot; then pull the needle through, holding the yarn until it must be released.

Fig. 10

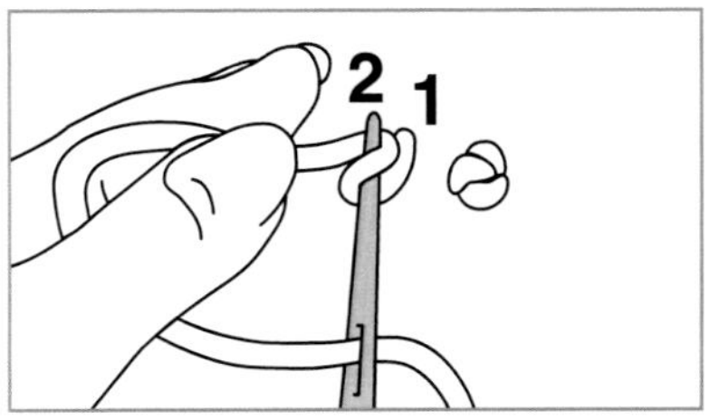

Straight Stitch

The straight stitch is just what the name implies, a single, straight stitch. Come up at 1 and go down at 2 ***(Fig. 11)***.

Fig. 11

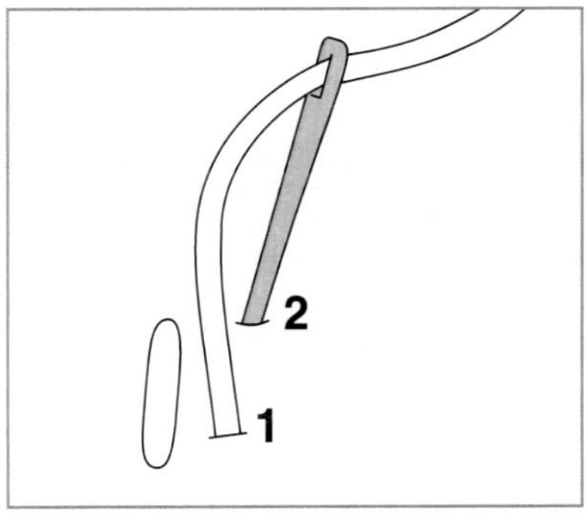

Basic Crochet Stitches

Single Crochet
(abbreviated sc)

Insert hook in stitch indicated, YO and pull up a loop, YO and draw through both loops on hook ***(Fig. 12)***.

Fig. 12

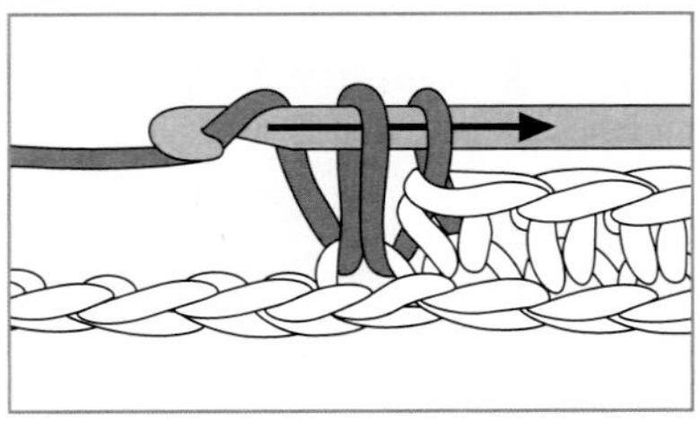

Half Double Crochet
(abbreviated hdc)

YO, insert hook in stitch indicated, YO and pull up a loop, YO and draw through all 3 loops on hook ***(Fig. 13)***.

Fig. 13

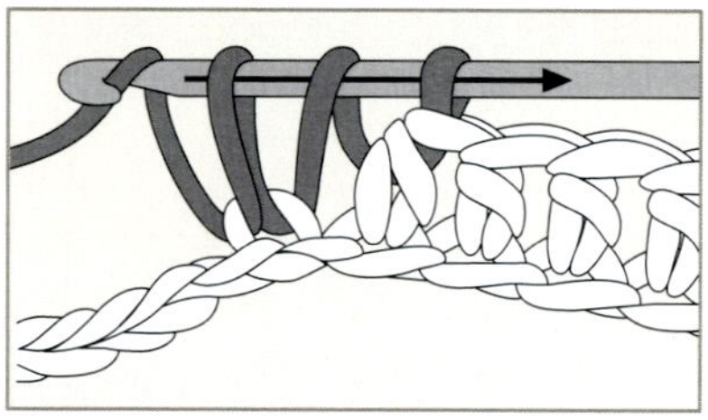

Double Crochet
(abbreviated dc)

YO, insert hook in next stitch, YO and pull up a loop (3 loops on hook), YO and draw through 2 loops on hook ***(Fig. 14a)***, YO and draw through remaining 2 loops on hook ***(Fig. 14b)***.

Fig. 14a

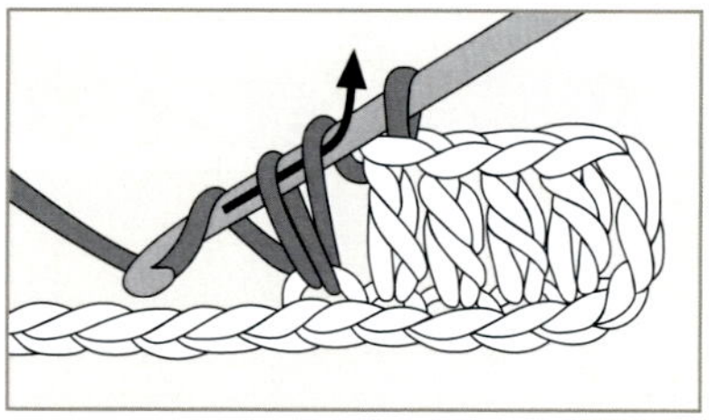

Fig. 14b

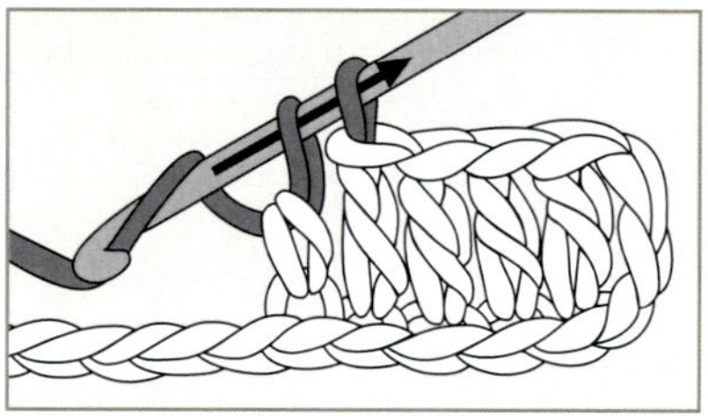

Treble Crochet
(abbreviated tr)

YO twice, insert hook in stitch indicated, YO and pull up a loop (4 loops on hook) ***(Fig. 15a)***, (YO and draw through 2 loops on hook) 3 times ***(Figs. 15b & c)***.

Fig.15a

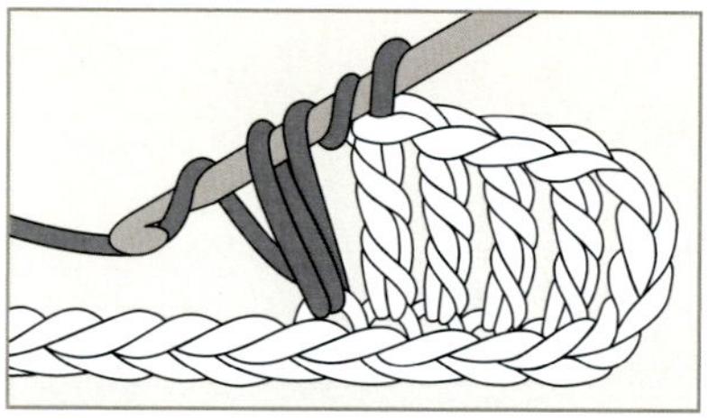

Fig. 15b

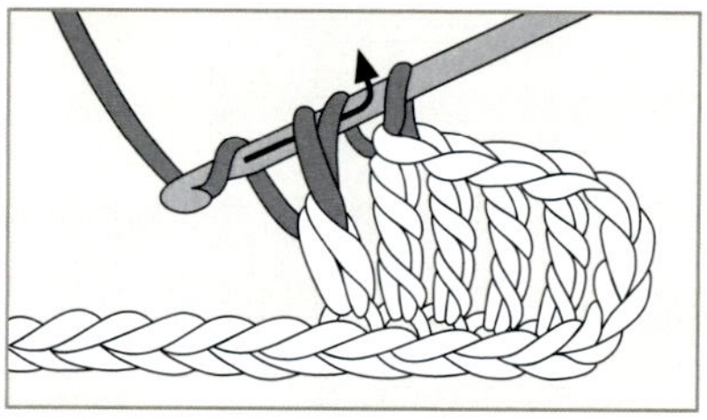

Fig. 15c

Double Treble Crochet
(abbreviated dtr)

YO 3 times, insert hook in stitch indicated, YO and pull up a loop (5 loops on hook) ***(Fig. 16)***, (YO and draw through 2 loops on hook) 4 times.

Fig. 16

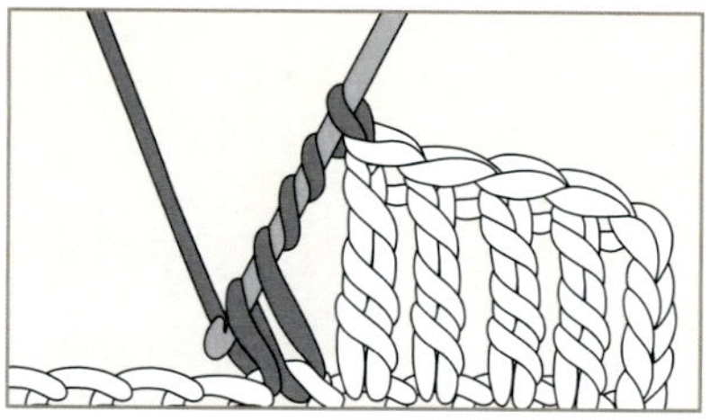

We have made every effort to ensure that these instructions are accurate and complete. We cannot, however, be responsible for human error, typographical mistakes, or variations in individual work.

Production Team: Project Manager/Technical Manager—Linda A. Daley;
Publishing Manager—Megan Copeland; Graphic Artist—Michael Douglas;
Photo Stylist—Lori Wenger; and Photographer—Jason Masters.

Made in U.S.A.